A CHAMPION'S GUIDE
To Thriving Beyond
Breast Cancer

D0733982

Praise for

A CHAMPION'S GUIDE
TO THRIVING BEYOND BREAST CANCER

"I am a breast cancer thriver since 1997. I wish I had read this book back then. This is a must read for anyone with breast cancer and their family. The author is really gifted and guided by God's love. The book is full of guidance and gives insight; it will help you and your loved ones. With the family also reading this book it will give them a better understanding of what you are going through and how they can help you."
—**Virginia M. Schindler**, Breast Cancer Thriver

"This book is an inspirational guide that provides hope and encouragement to those with breast cancer and their loved ones"
—**Kristin Shea**, RN OCN,
Florida Cancer Specialists & Research Center

"A Champion's Guide to Thriving Beyond Breast Cancer is a gift to all who must walk the path of cancer. I hope you will be as touched by this powerful book, as I have been. Let other women know about it."
—**Dr. Connie Hebert**, National Literacy Consultant
& Author of "The Teachable Minute"

"*This book is perfect for women going through a trial with breast cancer. It's wonderful, very encouraging, and very personal! God is spoken of throughout this book, and I know He's the most important ingredient to everyone's healing, strength, perseverance and hope as they walk through any trial.*"

—**Pam Kitchens**

"*What an amazing and enriching book! I learned so much from it.*" *I'm glad that He gave you the gift of time so that you can help millions of women to realize that they can be strivers, survivors and thrivers. I look forward to sharing your book.*"

—**Barbara Smith**

"*An uplifting, encouraging and empowering book. Stories of courage that are a must read for anyone on a journey with any type of cancer. I love the interactive study guide.*"

—**Whitney Chevtaikin**

"*A Champion's Guide To Thriving Beyond Breast Cancer is an inspiring and uplifting guide. I love the concept, and it's beautifully written. Janet I Mueller is such a fabulous author.*"

—**Natasha Jane Bullas,** Owner at Sun Coast Golf Center

A
CHAMPION'S
GUIDE
TO THRIVING BEYOND
BREAST CANCER

*Healing Stories for the Mind, Body and Soul, Giving You
Hope, Comfort, and Encouragement on Your Journey*

JANET I MUELLER

Kenosha Public Library
Kenosha, WI

3064513154664

A CHAMPION'S GUIDE TO THRIVING BEYOND BREAST CANCER
Healing Stories for the Mind, Body and Soul, Giving You
Hope, Comfort, and Encouragement on Your Journey

© 2014 JANET I MUELLER. All rights reserved.

No part of this publication may be reproduced or transmitted in any form or by any means, mechanical or electronic, including photocopying and recording, or by any information storage and retrieval system, without permission in writing from author or publisher (except by a reviewer, who may quote brief passages and/or show brief video clips in a review).

Disclaimer: The Publisher and the Author make no representations or warranties with respect to the accuracy or completeness of the contents of this work and specifically disclaim all warranties, including without limitation warranties of fitness for a particular purpose. No warranty may be created or extended by sales or promotional materials. The advice and strategies contained herein may not be suitable for every situation. This work is sold with the understanding that the Publisher is not engaged in rendering legal, accounting, or other professional services. If professional assistance is required, the services of a competent professional person should be sought. Neither the Publisher nor the Author shall be liable for damages arising herefrom. The fact that an organization or website is referred to in this work as a citation and/or a potential source of further information does not mean that the Author or the Publisher endorses the information the organization or website may provide or recommendations it may make. Further, readers should be aware that internet websites listed in this work may have changed or disappeared between when this work was written and when it is read.

ISBN 978-1-61448-630-5 paperback
ISBN 978-1-61448-631-2 eBook
Library of Congress Control Number: 2013931884

Morgan James Publishing
The Entrepreneurial Publisher
5 Penn Plaza, 23rd Floor
New York City, New York 10001
(212) 655-5470 office • (516) 908-4496 fax
www.MorganJamesPublishing.com

Cover Design by:
Rachel Lopez
www.r2cdesign.com

In an effort to support local communities, raise awareness and funds, Morgan James Publishing donates a percentage of all book sales for the life of each book to Habitat for Humanity Peninsula and Greater Williamsburg.

Get involved today, visit
www.MorganJamesBuilds.com.

Scripture quotations marked (AMP) are taken from the *Amplified Bible*, Copyright © 1954, 1958, 1962, 1964, 1965, 1987 by The Lockman Foundation.

Scripture quotations marked (ESV) are from The Holy Bible, English Standard Version® (ESV®), copyright © 2001 by Crossway, a publishing ministry of Good News Publishers. Used by permission. All rights reserved.

Scripture quotations marked (KJV) are taken from the King James Version

Scripture quotations marked (NIV) are taken from the Holy Bible, New International Version®, NIV®. Copyright © 1973, 1978, 1984 by Biblica, Inc.™ Used by permission of Zondervan. All rights reserved worldwide.

Scripture quotations marked (NLT) are taken from the Holy Bible, New Living Translation, copyright © 1996, 2004, 2007. Used by permission of Tyndale House Publishers, Inc., Carol Stream, Illinois 60188. All rights reserved.

copyright © 2012 J Mueller Group LLC

All rights reserved. No portion of this book may be reproduced in any form without the written consent of the Publisher.

Seminars by Janet I Mueller

Leadership In Excellence Academy™
Master The 7 C's To Personal Transformation™

For speaking, coaching and consulting
meet Janet online at

www.JanetIMueller.com

DEDICATED to my best friend, Judy Porter, whose life inspired me to write this book with His guidance. She lost her life to breast cancer at the age of just thirty-three. With eternal love and gratitude for the blessing of time He gave our friendship, and for placing such a beautiful person in my life. Her memory lives on in my heart forever.

My desire is that this book will serve to inspire, give hope, belief, and encourage you and women all around the world on their journey through and beyond breast cancer.

"Life is like the Olympics.
It's a series of events.
Run in such a way as to win the race.
You receive honor, victory,
and crowns for your accomplishments"
—Janet I. Mueller

TABLE OF CONTENTS

INTRODUCTION

In this book, *A Champion's Guide To Thriving Beyond Breast Cancer*, you will discover and learn how it is possible to thrive beyond breast cancer and other difficult life circumstances. This book was inspired through the loss of my best friend to breast cancer. My desire is that this book will serve you, inspire you, help you, give you hope, belief, and encourage you to have a Springboard Spirit. To have faith, stay in faith through and beyond your personal journey.

Women diagnosed with breast cancer often experience anxiety, depression, low self esteem, and identity issues that affect how they view themselves and others.

My vision is that this book will help you and millions of other women all around the world discover that it is possible to thrive beyond breast cancer. This book will teach you the importance of having:

- FAITH
- MINDSET
- BELIEF

In the pages ahead you will learn how other women have come through their journeys with breast cancer and other difficult life circumstances and are thriving beyond to tell their stories.

1

Here are encouraging facts as published in *Cancer Treatment and Survivorship Facts & Figures* 2012-2013. Atlanta: American Cancer Society; 2012.

As of January 1, 2022 it is estimated that:

- The population of cancer survivors will increase to almost 18 million of which 9.2 million are female.
- The number of female breast cancer survivors will be 3,786,610 (41%)

We cannot ignore the other facts that show:

- The estimated new cases of female breast cancer for 2012 is 226,870
- The median age for females diagnosed with breast cancer is age 61
- 20% of breast cancers occur in females younger than 50
- 40% of breast cancers occur in females older than 65

Think about other life circumstances you have thrived beyond. I'm sure you can relate to several as I can. Our lives are a tapestry of events. The truth is we know it is possible to live through and beyond life experiences and difficult circumstances. How? We know this because at some point or another throughout all of our lives that is exactly what we have done.

Personally, I have come through and thrived beyond several difficult and challenging life circumstances including my own dance with death. A near-death experience I survived that took place fifteen years ago. I'm here to tell you that it is possible. You can come through, rise above, and beyond this journey with breast cancer. As difficult as this may seem right now, more than ever you must be strong and believe with all your being that you will be victorious and win. Have faith that you will fulfill your heart's desires and accomplish your dreams in life. Think about all the reasons why you should thrive beyond this and think about all the people in your life who need you too.

Through the loss of my best friend to breast cancer, and my own personal life experiences, I set out on a mission to prove that it is possible to thrive beyond this journey. I went out into the community and interviewed seven women who are thriving beyond their personal journeys with breast cancer. My hope is that the stories in this book will serve you, inspire you, give you hope, and encourage you through and beyond your personal journey.

My message to you is *"This is your time, this is your time to thrive, this is your time to heal, this is your time to rise above these difficult and challenging life circumstances."*

Let's not look back, because we cannot change the past. We cannot go back. There's no point in regretting, beating ourselves up wishing we might have done things differently. It's not your fault, do not blame yourself; you did not ask for breast cancer. Instead look ahead and focus on the future. Set your sights on the finish line. Picture yourself crossing the finish line like an athlete.

Maybe you are taking this journey alone without close family or friends to support you. Perhaps you do not have the additional support you wished you had. Lean on this book, these stories to help you through and give you the encouragement, hope, and belief you need to triumph beyond.

Five years from now, how do you see your life? What are you doing, being, giving and celebrating? Whose life is different because of you? Whose life have you been able to impact as a result of thriving beyond this journey? Let's get started right now, and let me help you focus on thriving, not just surviving.

As we look at the facts, we see the improvements in survival rates; this is encouraging. Certainly early detection, widespread mammography screenings, and improvements in treatment are all key. I believe that it is also important to have faith, a positive mindset, and an unshakable belief that you can thrive beyond this journey. We see how this is demonstrated repeatedly throughout the stories in this book.

Think about the other times in your life when you have had to be strong and how you have come through and thrived beyond other life difficulties even though at the time they may have seemed near impossible. If you can do it once, you can do it again!

I'm certain, we all experience difficult times and it's no wonder we might ask questions like *"Why would this happen to me, I'm a good person."* Remember it's not what happens to you in life, it's what you do with it that counts. It's about who you become through the process. Maybe God's plan and purpose for you is that you go on in life to inspire, help and encourage others through and beyond their journey as a result of coming through and beyond your own. We all have a voice, a message to share. Your story can help someone else, you can write a book, share your message with others and serve them in their hours of need. It is my belief that we all have a purpose one far greater than just ourselves and that we are here to serve and help one another.

*For it is by grace you have been saved, through faith
and this is not from yourselves, it is the gift of God
not by works, so that no one can boast.*
—Ephesians 2:8-9 (NIV)

CHAPTER 1

A PASSPORT TO MORE TIME

JANET'S STORY

Fifteen years ago, while vacationing on the island of Fuerteventura in the Canary Islands off the coast of North Africa, I survived a near-death experience. I was attacked by a stranger and found myself in a nonnegotiable position with a razor blade held at my neck. I vividly recall in that moment praying, *"Dear God, please don't let me die!"* During the attack I saw my entire life flash by in seconds, like a movie on fast-forward. I remember thinking, *"There's so much more I want to do. Please, dear God, don't let me die. I am not ready."*

My biggest struggle for a long time following the event was that *I had no control over the situation.* I was forced to accept the fact that bad things do happen to good people, even though we don't understand why.

By the grace of God I am here today, and for that I am eternally grateful. He gave me a passport to live beyond my life circumstances and blessed me with a gift of more time to help and serve others in this world. I feel deeply blessed for this gift because it led me to a beautiful friendship with Judy Porter, who would in time become my best friend in the world. This rich friendship was born and blossomed from God's favor.

What I learned through my near-death experience was that we should live each day as though it were our last by being present with those we love, giving to others more fully, and living life in a much more meaningful way. We should be grateful for all our joys in life and have faith, believing that He has a bigger plan for each one of us, even though we may not understand what that plan is. We must trust that we are on this path right now for a reason. His purpose for all our lives is revealed in time, His time.

I believe that I am here to help and serve others in whatever ways God wants me to. I feel a much deeper sense of gratitude for life, and I cherish and guard my time more so than I did before. I received a wake-up call as to just how precious life is and what a blessing it is. I am forever grateful for the wonderful friendship Judy and I shared. She was such a beautiful person and meant the world to me.

Judy always encouraged me to pursue my dreams and to go after a bigger vision despite life's circumstances. I am grateful to her for all her encouragement. In pursuit of an excellent life, I purchased a one-way ticket and boarded the plane bound for the United States two years following my near-death experience to begin a lifelong dream.

Across the ocean, our friendship continued to blossom. I am grateful for the fun memories we created during our trips to visit one another back and forth between the UK and Florida.

Unfortunately Judy did not live beyond breast cancer. At the young age of just thirty-three, a daughter, wife, mother, and my best friend was called by Him and went to heaven.

I felt called to write this book and have been guided throughout its entire creation. The calling said, *"Help millions of women all around the world!"*

I believe God wants to show you his favor and that you should expect great things.

JUDY PORTER

CHAPTER 2

A BLESSING AND
AN INSPIRATION

JUDY'S STORY
A SEVENTH YEAR CELEBRATION

She stood quietly in the corner, alone and looking shy and kind of awkward as I recall. She looked like a fish out of water.

I remember feeling compassion and sadness as I wondered why no one was talking to her. I walked over to her to say hi.

It was 1996, and this was my first big corporate meeting in my new job with Avon, UK. I was excited I had finally landed the job of my dreams after 12 months of going through a series of interviews. My boss to be, who became a wonderful mentor to me, was initially concerned with my tender age even though I was a mature and responsible young woman and I wasn't afraid of hard work. I became the youngest member of the management team.

I watched as the old-timers and social butterflies rallied around one another, chatting and being careful not to spill their tea.

Judy was wearing a black skirt suit and it matched her hair color perfectly. Her rich toffee brown eyes twinkled back at me as I went to greet her and said *"Hi, how are you? My name is Janet."* We shook hands and she smiled back at me and said, *"Hi, my name is Judy, Judy Porter. How are you doing?"*

Sometimes you meet someone and you just hit it off. The conversation was easy and had rhythm. Like a pendulum swinging back and forth effortlessly.

In time, Judy became my best friend in the whole world. I'd describe her as an introvert really. She was on the quieter side and so was I. We hit it off perfectly even though they say opposites attract, they also say like attracts like.

Our friendship blossomed as we took our journey together in our new jobs as area sales managers. Working for Avon, we had the pleasure of helping 10 or more women each week get started in their own home based business giving them an opportunity to improve their lives and earn extra income. In some cases the women we helped were able to change their lives radically as a result of their new business.

Judy and I would delight in meeting for lunch sometimes during our busy workweek and we'd laugh, swap stories about our days, and talked about the wins and challenges we both encountered along the way. I remember this one particular English pub we would go to that served a great lunch menu. It was conveniently located half way between our two territories. She loved to order pizza, one of her favorite things in the world.

I recall one particularly snowy and cold day sitting in my car, freezing and hugging a flask of hot coffee. I was looking out the car window after knocking on doors all morning, trying to get warm and wishing I didn't have to go out there again in that bitter cold weather. If I was to recruit ten people this week then that's what I would do.

Before I did, I thought, "*I know I'll call Judy to see how her day is going.*" I wondered if, like me, she sat in her car somewhere freezing and hugging a flask of coffee trying to stay warm.

I called, and she answered the phone in her usual light and friendly tone. "*Hey, you. Whatcha doing? Where are you?*"

I said "*Oh, I'm sitting in my car freezing cold in Leeds, and I really don't want to go out in all this snow again. How about you? What are you doing?*"

"*What am I doing? Take a guess… I'm home sitting in front of the lovely warm fire, having a cup of tea and a biscuit watching TV.*"

"*What?*" I asked, laughing so hard I nearly dropped the flask of coffee on the floor. Did she just say what I thought she said? She was at home sitting in front of a nice warm fire having tea?

Here came the confirmation…"*Yeah, I'm home and it's nice and warm in here. Getcha self home, girl. What are you doing running around like a madwoman in all that snow?*"

This is what I loved about my best friend: her sense of humor, her carefree attitude, and her ability to be so laid back. You could say she was so laid back she'd fall over.

Either she'd already recruited ten people for the week or couldn't be bothered. All I knew was that she was at home sipping hot tea in front of the fire and I was outside in the snow freezing.

Judy had such a carefree attitude and probably the funniest sense of humor I've ever come across. If your personalities clicked, she was the kind of person who could have you in stitches laughing your you know what off in no time flat and without even trying.

Judy's boyfriend Michael loved to surf and cycle. When he went on his trips she and I would hang out, go to the movies or out for dinner.

She'd make fun of how hard I worked. She'd say things like, "*What the heck are you doing putting all these hours in, you silly cow?*" Now "*silly cow*" said in a British sarcastic way sounds much better than you probably imagine it would. It was really said in a loving, affectionate kind of way; a way that only Judy could say it. You knew she was coming from a place of love.

Beneath her shyness she was a sensitive, loving, and caring woman. Often misunderstood as I came to realize. I think introverts are misunderstood. They are perceived as being different.

I know she loved her only son, Elliott. Actually, I remember getting the call, the call that changed the world as she knew it then. She had called and said, "*Pull over. I need to speak to you. I'm pregnant. I am going to have a baby.*" I couldn't believe it. My best friend was about to become a mother. It all seemed very grown up. Now this was when we were younger of course. She was excited and so I was absolutely thrilled for her.

We had grown up in different towns, she in Bradford and I in Halifax. Both of us were from middle-class working families. I remember telling her about my dream for a better life, to emigrate to America. While most people laughed at my idea, she didn't. She never did. She would encourage me. She'd say things like, "*You go for it, girl. Why not? Yeah, I'll miss 'ya, but go.*"

Our friendship continued across the ocean. She came over to visit me several times and really loved it here in Florida. It was almost New Year's Eve the Millennium and I got a call from Judy and she said, "*I know this is a crazy idea, it's only a few days away, but what do you think about meeting me in Miami for New Year's Eve?*"

I said, "*What do I think? Are you nuts?*" I'd embrace any chance to see my best friend at New Year, or anytime for that matter! If she can travel across the ocean for eight or nine hours, I can most definitely make the seven-hour drive from Gainesville to Miami.

We met for the millennium in Miami and had an absolute ball.

My work continued with Avon in the United States for many years following my departure from the UK. Judy's career however, took on a new path. She went on to higher education and graduated with her degree. I remember the photograph she sent me. She looked radiant in her black cap and gown, holding her certificate with pride and smiling widely. I was so very proud of her.

Judy had parted from her boyfriend Michael, Elliott's dad, and had fallen head-over-heels for her husband-to-be, Brian. I didn't really know him except for the brief time we had together when the two of them visited my husband and me in Florida.

I'd often call Judy on the weekend and we'd chat for hours. One particular February morning when I called, I felt like I'd been hit by a train, all the wind knocked out of me. The news I received was shocking. Judy had been diagnosed with breast cancer. I could tell she felt uncomfortable and didn't want to explain it all in great detail. I was deeply saddened by the news yet my heart was hopeful.

A few months later, in May, my family and I took a trip to England to be with her. When we arrived at Judy's house, her mom greeted us and anxiously told us Judy had been admitted to the hospital. I got into the car immediately with her mom, and we raced to see her. My husband and daughter stayed at the house and were understandably tired following a nine-hour flight.

I was not prepared to see what I saw nor had I been told just how late-stage Judy's breast cancer was. As I stood at the entrance of her room I hesitated and prayed she'd look fine. I was afraid to go in and see her. Entering the hospital room I saw my best friend sitting on the bed. My intuition was right. I barely recognized her and I did everything I could to hold back the tears.

"*Hey, you, how are you?*" I said, as I gave her the biggest hug ever. She said, "*I'm fine, Janet. How are you doing?*"

She didn't look fine to me at all. My best friend didn't look anything like she had just a few years earlier. In fact I hardly recognized her. The cancer had spread from her breast to her brain.

Judy had asked that I bring with me from home a particular photograph I had of her. I gave it to her at the hospital and this had made her happy. She commented *"I look good in this picture don't I?"* A few days later Judy was released from hospital and went home.

We were out to dinner one evening. Judy kept saying she wanted to go back with me to Florida. *"I just want to be with you,"* she said, *"so we can hang out. That's where I want to be."* I felt deep inside like my best friend was warning me she was leaving me.

She wanted to get away, away from it all, and I wanted so desperately to rescue her and make it all just go away. So I said to her, *"Come on. Come back with me, Judy. You can."* In my heart, I had this feeling, I knew. I believe she wanted to spend her last days here, in the sunshine with people who loved her.

The next evening we were at Judy's house, and I thought about ways in which I could comfort her, I thought she might like a massage or manicure so I offered to give her a pampering session. I painted her nails and gave her tiny massages. Afterwards, she held my daughter Daniella and said how incredibly beautiful she was.

The day of our departure had arrived way too soon, a day I was not looking forward to because somewhere deep within me I knew this was the very last time I would see my best friend. I did my best to be brave but couldn't any longer. I lost it.

My family and I drove up and down the street several times as I tried to stop crying. I couldn't let Judy see my hurt. I didn't want her to see or sense it. I didn't want her to know that I knew. I wanted to give her hope. I wanted to believe, and for her to believe, that we would see each other again soon.

I remember hugging Judy so hard and not wanting to let her go. I couldn't bear the thought of leaving her and never seeing her or hearing her voice again. How could I just get back on a plane and leave my best friend like this? I felt helpless and also guilty, guilty that I was living when I knew she was dying.

During the next few months we spoke often. Then as time went on, whenever I called her, I was told she was unable to come to the phone, she was in bed.

In August of that same year, I got the call I had known was coming and didn't want to answer. My best friend, Judy, had died at the age of thirty-three from breast cancer, and there wasn't a damn thing I could do about it.

Today, I celebrate Judy's life and acknowledge the seven years since her passing. I am incredibly blessed that she and I were best friends, and I am thankful to God that He placed such a beautiful person in my life, a person whose life will live on in my heart forever and who inspired me to write this book.

It is my desire that the stories in this book will give you hope and will encourage you on your journey through and beyond breast cancer.

It is possible to thrive beyond our life circumstances, as I have done and as have the women who share their stories in this book.

My desire is that you, too, will go forward through and beyond your journey and thrive!

Jesus turned and saw her.
"Take heart, daughter," he said,
"your faith has healed you."
And the woman was healed at that moment.
—Matthew 9:22 (NIV)

CHAPTER 3

A SPRINGBOARD SPIRIT

An athlete, a champion has a Springboard Spirit. A Springboard Spirit is one of faith. It is positive and is not defeated. It is not defined by life circumstance. It is courageous it bounces back and is bold. It perseveres, endures and doesn't give up. It presses forward, through, and beyond difficulty. Its focus is on the future not the past. It forgives and is free to move forward and beyond. It is hopeful. It keeps the desires and goals in life alive. A Springboard Spirit runs to win; it is a victor not a victim. It is like a wild stallion full of spirit. It fights the good fight. It doesn't give up. It is strong. It is a Springboard Spirit. A Springboard Spirit thrives beyond life's difficulties.

The three B's of a Springboard Spirit are:

BE BOLD · BE BRAVE · BE BEAUTIFUL

FOUR PILLARS TO
A SPRINGBOARD SPIRIT

I - FAITH

For nothing is impossible with God
—Luke 1:37 (ESV)

II - MIND

For I know the plans I have for you, declares the Lord,
"plans to prosper you and not to harm you,
plans to give you hope and a future."
—Jeremiah 29:11 (NIV)

III - BODY

He gives strength to the weary and increases the power of the weak.
Even youths grow tired and weary, and young men stumble and fall;
but those who hope in the Lord will renew their strength.
They will soar on wings like eagles; they will run and not grow weary,
they will walk and not be faint.
—Isaiah 40:29-31 (NIV)

IV – SOUL

He restores my soul.
He guides me in paths of righteousness
for his name's sake.
—Psalm 23:3 (NIV84)

PILLAR I - FAITH

He is a merciful, compassionate, caring, and never-changing God. Therefore He can do now what He has done before.

Stay in faith and be bold in your prayers to Him. Ask Him to propel you into a place beyond your present life circumstances, a place where you are thriving and healed beyond breast cancer.

Ask with confidence for His favor and deliverance, not with doubt. Remember He loves each and every one of us equally. He has a plan and purpose for all our lives. He is in charge. It's His will, not ours.

"*Then why doesn't He heal everyone?*" you might ask. My answer to you is, "*I don't know. I do know that He has the power and a will.*"

I encourage you to be willing to strengthen your faith and your relationship with Him. Spend time each day reading the Bible, and getting in agreement with Him.

Believe that He has the power to heal you. This is the same never-changing God who has raised children from the dead, made blind men see, and helped the lame to walk. Isn't it possible then that He can also provide healing to you? I did not state or promise that He would, for we do not know His will. Only He knows. I'm asking if you think it's possible for him to heal you.

I am not suggesting that you sit back and wait for a miraculous healing, although that could happen. By all means you should receive the treatments and medical care you need and have decided upon. What I am saying is do not underestimate the power of our almighty God. Stay in faith.

PILLAR II - MIND

I understand how difficult it may seem to remain positive and upbeat especially when faced with life's difficulties and circumstances, I do. You mustn't let these circumstances steal your joy, and certainly do not let them defeat you or define you. I know that you didn't ask for this disease of the flesh. You are not your cancer.

Do not blame yourself for it either because that is not going to serve you on your road to recovery. Bad things happen to good people all the time, and it's difficult to understand why that is. Trust that He has a higher purpose, a bigger plan for you.

Decide that cancer will not beat you. It's not the spirit of who you are. You must try to remain as positive as you possibly can during this journey. As difficult as this may sound, I do believe that what we think is meant to harm us will be used for our good. Often out of the most difficult of life circumstances come new blessings. You will see these blessings, the blessings each woman feels she has received as a result of her journey through and beyond breast cancer, shared throughout the stories in this book.

Make the decision today to focus your mind and energy with the expectation of having the best possible outcome in this situation.

Be steadfast in your faith, and do not let your heart and mind be troubled. Rise above and beyond this stormy season in life. Have peace knowing that God has you in the palm of his hand.

Picture yourself at the end of this journey, thriving beyond breast cancer. Turn your attention and energy towards thriving instead of surviving. It is a journey and you will endure. You will and must persevere. You will need to be strong and have courage. You must believe it is possible for you to win this race and run farther than you think you can, run to win and envision yourself crossing over the finish line.

Do not give in or give up on the dreams and desires in your heart. Remember He sees your heart and knows all your desires. Stay in faith and believe you will accomplish them.

Be hopeful and see yourself living your heart's desires, living a life beyond this season of inconvenience. Do not let these circumstances cause you to give up hope, lose faith, or compromise your dreams in life.

Our Lord Almighty has supernatural powers and we know, according to what the Bible says, that He can provide healing. Since He is a never-changing God, do you think it is possible that he can heal you?

PILLAR III - BODY

See yourself as an athlete a champion. Picture yourself strong, healthy, full of energy, and courageous. Winning this fight. You are a victor not a victim.

Do not allow the weakness or inconvenience of the body dampen or crush your spirit. Keep your spirit high. Just like an athlete, know that you can overcome, endure, persevere, and come through your journey from start to finish and accomplish victory.

As a girl, I dedicated ten years to gymnastics, a sport I loved. I remember falling off the beam many times and bruising my shinbones to the point that they were black-and-blue, tender to the touch. Boy did it hurt! I learned that I had to take tiny bold steps from one end of the beam to the other. Five days a week of rigorous training and exercise left me with aching muscles that didn't have time to recover from one day's training to the next.

I don't suppose my fear of heights served me too well either as a gymnast, although I loved the sport. I recall one time when I simply froze on the high bar just as I was about to try a new move. I knew at any moment I could fall and get injured. Somehow I finally mustered the courage and pushed beyond the fear to tackle the move.

Do not let your circumstances and journey through breast cancer defeat you. Be courageous and keep your desires and passions alive. Do not give up. See yourself as the athlete winning the race.

PILLAR IV - SOUL

The soul is the spiritual part of each of us, the part that does not die. Just like a delicious apple, we each have a center or core. Our spirit is the sheer pure essence of who we are. Obedient, strong willed, feisty, combative, and testy are all words sometimes used to describe a person's spirit. When it comes to your spirit in regard to thriving beyond breast cancer, my hope is that you have the spirit of a wild stallion and refuse to have your spirit broken. Have a Springboard Spirit!

In faith I hope that your will is softened and becomes His will instead.

It is so important, especially during life's difficulties and times of turbulence, that we each find our place of peace, that internal place of peace and comfort. This is the place where our faith lives. It is a place of truth, a place of whom and what we are, and what our heart desires. It is an innocent and pure place that is deep within each of us, a childlike place where life experience hasn't jaded us. It is a place known and seen by God himself.

I want to share with you a journey I traveled recently; I arrived at a place that felt like home to me. I believe the Holy Spirit was with me on this journey, and I don't use the term Holy Spirit lightly. This experience occurred after most of this book had already been written, and it was only after discussing it with my pastor that I realized what it was that I had experienced.

I should also confess that, while I have no recollection of being introduced to the church as a child, I always believed in God and prayed. I have no question that He is real and all around us and that He speaks to us. In my final few days completing this book, He told me I wasn't finished, and that I needed to rewrite one third or so of the pages in it. What I proceeded to write may make you think I have been a strong, deep-faith Christian my whole life who has a relationship with God, a real relationship.

Here is how the first part of the journey unfolded.

As I lay resting one evening I felt totally at peace, and a sense of pure joy and rejuvenation came over me. As I closed my eyes, I saw a place that looks and feels like home to me, a familiar place. It looked like a beautiful, serene place like one I have visited often for vacation. It looked like the Greek Islands.

I see myself in a room, laying down and dressed in a white chiffon nightgown, with crisp white cotton sheets, and sheer white curtains blowing gently in the wind. I feel a warm breeze caress my face as I lay peacefully listening to the sound of the ocean waves gently lapping back and forth. I see myself with my natural long and dark hair. I feel totally at peace, calm and full of joy.

I felt as though I had been touched in a warm and special way in my heart, in my soul. I see myself getting up from my rest, and looking out beyond the open doors, admiring the ocean view and beautiful white buildings. I feel rejuvenated, whole, and healed.

What an incredible and beautiful experience this was!

My desire for you is that you too will experience such a wonderful moment and will journey to your place of peace and healing. I ask that you pray to Him that you are thriving beyond breast cancer. He has the power to provide healing.

He guided my steps and turned this inspirational self-help book into one of faith also. I believe He wants you to deepen your relationship with Him.

He took her by the hand and said to her,
"Talitha koum!"
(which means "Little girl, I say to you, get up!")
—Mark 5:41 (NIV)

A SPRINGBOARD SPIRIT
SEVEN DAILY AFFIRMATIONS

Seven daily affirmations to uplift and encourage you on your journey through and beyond breast cancer.

1. I am keeping my heart's desires alive and will not let my circumstances defeat me.
2. I am competing to win and see myself crossing the finish line, accomplishing victory beyond breast cancer.
3. I am courageous and I will keep focused on my heart's desires and will not let breast cancer stand in my way.
4. I am taking bold steps throughout my journey.
5. I will get up every time if I should fall.
6. I will persevere and keep going even when it seems difficult; I will not quit.
7. I can see myself thriving beyond my circumstances, accomplishing victory, and living my heart's desires. I have a heart of hope, and I will stay in faith.

Action Step
Find a photograph of yourself looking your most healthy and radiant and put it where you will see it every day as a reminder of the outcome you desire.

TAMMY

And the peace of God,
which surpasses all understanding,
will guard your hearts and minds through Christ Jesus.
—Philippians 4:7 (KJV)

CHAPTER 4

A BLANKET OF PEACE

TAMMY'S STORY

T ammy is a five-year breast cancer thriver. She is a beautiful, radiant, and kind-hearted woman of faith. Tammy was born and raised in Ocala, Florida, where she worked in banking and administration. Following her successful treatment for breast cancer, she went on to attend a local support group, where she provided mentoring, support, and acted as a sounding board for other women with breast cancer.

Tammy comes from a long line of strong, positive, and faith-filled women. She shares how her own mother's faith brought about healing in her life. While there was no history of breast cancer in Tammy's immediate family, she does recall that two of her great aunts and a cousin had it.

Now, through Tammy's personal journey and experience with and beyond breast cancer, she too, steps out as a woman of strength, continuing the family legacy of deep-rooted faith. Tammy is grateful that she was diagnosed early with stage 1 ductal carcinoma in situ breast cancer and believes she was greatly blessed for receiving timely care.

Tammy feels that mammography diagnostic screening literally helped save her life because her tumor was buried so deep within her chest wall that it could not have been detected through self-examination.

On May 11, 2007 she had a biopsy and three days later Tammy received the news, it was confirmed she had breast cancer.

Tammy, who was then just forty-five and a stay-at-home mom of twelve months, recalls how the conversation on the phone started positive and upbeat. She felt for sure that it was going to be good news, but in just moments her whole world was turned upside down. Tammy was overwhelmed by the feelings and whirlwind chain of events she experienced over the next several days and in the weeks that followed.

Tammy recalls how she wept upon hearing the diagnosis. Continuing the drive to school, she called a close friend and told her the news.

Her friend shared Psalm 118:7, which declares life and not death. After Tammy dropped her son off at preschool, she gathered with four of her friends, who shared their compassion as they prayed over her.

On her drive to meet her husband, Tammy declared aloud in the car, repeating several times over:

"I will live; I will not die, in Jesus's name," as if it was already so. *"I know this is not your plan for me."*

Tammy and her husband went to the surgeon's office together to discuss next steps. She also wanted to make sure her sister, who worked there, did not see the pathology report before Tammy had a chance to talk to her first. The surgeon advised Tammy to schedule appointments with the oncologist and radiation oncologist.

Tammy also had an MRI, taking a prescribed relaxant to combat the claustrophobic feelings that she, like many women, expected to experience.

When it came time to tell their son, Michael, Tammy remembers how she and her husband were open and truthful about what was happening. While careful to instill confidence, they laid out what would happen next and what care Mommy would need. In relating to their young child, they found it helpful to share with him the Berenstain Bears children's book in which the young bear would experience surgery. As parents they felt this would make it easier for their son Michael, to relate to the situation.

A few days later, on May 17th, 2007, Tammy underwent a lumpectomy and the removal of several lymph nodes.

Tammy recalls how during the week of diagnosis, appointments, tests, and surgery an overwhelming peace covered her and her family. This feeling is not easy for her to explain. She says it felt tangible, like a huge soft blanket. It was the peace of God, and His peace carried them through this difficult time.

"*This is just a speed bump*," Tammy told herself. "*We will come through and over this. Let's get on with it.*"

Tammy opted for radiation treatment. As a result she went through thirty-three rounds of full-breast radiation. Initially her hopes were high for having radiation delivered directly to the area surrounding where the tumor had been, a treatment called mammosite radiation.

Her love for her heavenly Father had restored her. Tammy's deep faith built on a rock, not sand, would not be shaken even though the storm had come. It would not break her. She felt peace from Him.

There were three times during Tammy's journey with breast cancer when doubts entered her mind. She recalls how she awoke one night and found herself looking around the living room at all the family photographs. She held her gaze upon a photo of her son, pleading and asking God why. Why would He bring in this wonderful blessing, a son who was born to her finally after seven years, and then have Tammy leave him?

From that moment on she focused on many of the healing scriptures in the Bible. She says that reading scripture literally became her additional prescribed medicine, and it helped her so much.

Tammy shares how the Bible teaches us about making the right choices. "*You can choose life or you can choose death,*" she says. "*I wasn't going to bury my head in the sand like an ostrich. I chose life. I wasn't going to own cancer; it was not my cancer.*"

Tammy did not let cancer define who she is or let it defeat her.

As Tammy celebrates her five-year victory beyond breast cancer, she shares how every day is such a blessing, a true gift from God. She chooses to focus her days pouring out love and help and lifting others up, always remaining positive and choosing to see the good whenever possible.

"*Time is our currency, and we must spend it wisely,*" she says. "*It is a gift from God.*"

Tammy is so grateful to Him for his unconditional love and for granting her more time. God is a creator, but He did not create the cancer. He delivered her, saved her, and was her tower of refuge.

Today, Tammy's hope is that she can be the eyes, ears, hands, and mouthpiece for His good work, to help others in their times of need as a way to show her immense gratitude and appreciation to Him for his gift of deliverance. She feels blessed to help families, parents, and children in her daily work as office coordinator and registrar.

Tammy's message to you as she reaches out her hand is, "*You don't need to walk this journey alone. He will carry you. His plans and thoughts for you are higher than your own.*"

Tammy shares her three important anchors in life:

FAITH

FAMILY

FRIENDS

Tammy also shares how the breast cancer diagnosis affects the entire family and those close to them, not just the person receiving the diagnosis. It truly is a family matter and each family member or friend is affected by the news differently, something to be conscious of since this can affect how others respond to you during your time of need. They too, are faced with many emotions and thoughts about the situation.

As Tammy reflects on her journey of breast cancer and beyond she says that she can't imagine coming through and beyond it as a five-year thriver without the love of her family and friends and without the grace of God.

For I know the thoughts and plans that I have for you,
says the Lord,
thoughts and plans for welfare and peace and not for evil,
to give you hope in your final outcome.
—Jeremiah 29:11 (AMP)

Coaching Insights

1. What did you find most inspiring about Tammy's story?

2. What was it about her attitude, faith, and mindset that stood out to you the most?

3. How is her story similar to yours?

4. How is it different?

5. What did you learn from reading her story?

6. What part of her story did you find uplifting and comforting?

7. What are the three biggest takeaways you got from her story?

Your Notes...

MARTHA

Be on your guard;
stand firm in the faith;
be courageous; be strong.
—1 Corinthians 16:13 (NIV)

CHAPTER 5

A STRONG GIRL'S RACE

MARTHA'S STORY

M artha is a lively, beautiful, upbeat, and positive woman, a mother to three grown children and grandmother to eight wonderful grandchildren. She went skydiving on her fiftieth birthday, and loves to swim with dolphins. At the age of sixty-two she completed the Iron Girl Triathlon.

This woman of courage, strength, and inspiration tells me: "*I don't do sad.*"

Martha describes herself as a fairly private person, an independent woman who likes to be in control and who is more than capable of taking care of herself. Many of today's women are likeminded and share Martha's independence and self-reliance.

When she was sixty Martha was diagnosed with stage 1 breast cancer.

I believe that each woman's reaction to hearing the words *"you have breast cancer"* is personal; it's not one size fits all. Each woman may respond in a different way.

Martha recalls receiving her diagnosis when she was on her way out the door to a hair appointment. She felt she needed some quiet time to process the news and decided to share it only with her immediate family, including her husband, children, and sister.

"Knowledge is power," Martha says.

She found herself researching and learning as much as she could about the disease. She says she hadn't really known anyone with breast cancer. There wasn't any family history of the disease, and her mammograms had been negative for the previous fifteen years. By learning more about the disease, she could be informed and have a deeper understanding of it.

What appeared to be simply part of the fatty tissue in her right breast turned out to be stage 1 breast cancer, a tumor 0.7 cm in size. The lump was discovered on April 1, 2008, April Fools' Day. It had not been discovered during examinations when Martha was lying down, and it hadn't shown on the mammogram. The lump could only be felt when she was sitting or standing.

Martha says she is grateful that her physician took such a proactive approach toward her care and that her breast cancer was diagnosed early. Her general surgeon suggested she have a core needle biopsy, but Martha asked to have an excisional biopsy instead.

Martha's physician presented her with various treatment options, and ultimately it was a personal decision. She decided to have a bilateral mastectomy and reconstructive surgery. She felt this was the best option for her and her safest bet.

This is not the decision that all women might make. Nevertheless this was the best decision for Martha, and today she has no regrets.

As I mentioned earlier it's your decision what course of treatment to pursue, and you have to do what you feel is best for you. Be informed, ask questions, know your treatment options, and if necessary be willing to seek a second opinion. You must take a proactive role in your own care and treatment.

Martha shares her gratitude that she was diagnosed at an early stage and that the lump was relatively small.

On June 3, 2008, Martha underwent surgery and was literally up and running just three months later, completing the thirty-mile Atlanta 2-Day Walk for Breast Cancer. This was such a triumph, especially since pre-breast cancer Martha didn't like to sweat or run and hadn't really been athletic at all.

Martha's advice to other women who choose reconstructive surgery is, "*Make sure you consult with several plastic surgeons before reconstruction if that's your choice.*"

In June 2009, only five months after getting a clean bill of health, Martha went on to complete the Iron Girl Sprint Triathlon in Atlanta to celebrate her one-year anniversary as a breast cancer survivor.

Throughout Martha's breast cancer experience, her children were her biggest inspiration. They were her Why, her drive, her reason for getting through her disease. She recalls how one of her daughters, Lauren, stayed by her side for twenty-four hours after surgery and what a comfort that was.

I think as strong and independent as we might like to see ourselves as women; there comes a time that we all need a helping hand, someone to provide support and comfort. There is no shame in this.

Learning and blessings often come through experiencing the most difficult of times. One of the biggest blessings Martha says she received from having breast cancer is that she has made some amazing friends, in fact best friends or as Martha refers to them, breast friends.

Martha shares how she and her friends Debbie and Debbie, whom she refers to as the Little Debbies, like to get together a couple of times each month for lunch at different restaurants. The three of them spend time laughing and sharing their stories, which often extends into late afternoon. They have come together and their friendship has blossomed as a result of what once began as each one's individual journey with breast cancer.

Martha says, "*You are part of a sisterhood. Perhaps not one you may have wanted to join consciously, but nonetheless you are part of a group of extraordinary and powerful women.*"

Martha recalls another blessing that came after surgery, and how happy she was to follow her doctor's orders pertaining to household chores. "*I didn't have to vacuum, cook, or clean,*" she laughs.

I think, as women, we spend so much time nurturing and taking care of everyone else's needs—often trying to be all things to all people—that we find ourselves running around like a headless chicken. What we must learn to do or remind ourselves to do is take great care of us, too. This means that we should take time to stop and smell the roses, slow down, and appreciate life, family, and friends more fully in a vibrant way.

After all, you cannot give what you do not have. We must take time to pour water back into the pail, to fill it up to overflowing so we have something left to give to others.

Today Martha enjoys gardening, and she delights in sharing with me about her thirty-six rose bushes. Her days start out calmer now, she says. Rising early, she takes her morning coffee and sits for a while on the patio enjoying reading her daily journal and daily devotions. She follows her quiet time with a three-mile walk through the rolling hills of her neighborhood.

She enjoys listening to Christian rock and tells me how she feels her faith has strengthened significantly through and beyond her diagnosis with breast cancer.

Martha's increased awareness and purposeful decisions have led to a healthy lifestyle, including eating nutritious foods, staying hydrated, and exercising regularly. She walks five times a week, and if the weather is bad stays active by doing kickboxing in her home.

Through Martha's own personal journey with breast cancer, she was inspired to write the book Pink Lemonade.

She is also a member of the National Speaker's Association and former president of the group's Georgia chapter. Martha loves speaking and sharing her message of hope, inspiring others to overcome their challenges and enjoy life.

"All I could think about was living."
—Martha

Coaching Insights

1. What did you find most inspiring about Martha's story?

2. What was it about her attitude, faith, and mindset that stood out to you the most?

3. How is her story similar to yours?

4. How is it different?

5. What did you learn from reading her story?

6. What part of her story did you find uplifting and comforting?

7. What are the three biggest takeaways you got from her story?

Your Notes...

ANGELA

Love each other with genuine affection,
and take delight in honoring each other.
—Romans 12:10 (NLT)

CHAPTER 6

A DESIRE IN MY HEART

ANGELA'S STORY

Angela is an attractive, brave woman with a heart of gold. She is a business owner; wife to Brian, her high school sweetheart; and mother to their two children, a boy and a girl. Angela was diagnosed with stage 2 breast cancer at the young age of thirty-five.

Originally from Ohio, Angela now lives with her family in Florida, where she leads an active lifestyle and stays busy with her business. She shares how she led what she would consider a relatively healthy lifestyle prior to her diagnosis of breast cancer.

At the time of Angela's diagnosis, she was a stay-at-home mom. Her son was in kindergarten, and she filled her days with looking after and entertaining her then two-year-old daughter. Angela felt that life was good.

Then whilst taking a shower one day, Angela noticed something unusual as she performed her breast self-exam. She tried to stay positive and not worry too much about it, even though in her gut she had a deep nagging and gnawing feeling that something wasn't right. A few months later, her gynecologist performed a clinical exam and told Angela to get a baseline mammogram.

As many stay-at-home moms know only too well, it is easy to lose track of time when you are busy catering to the demands of young children, doing household chores, and running errands. Time passed and the days turned into weeks, until another day while showering Angela noticed a significant change in the appearance of her breast. The nipple was now facing in a different direction! This change quickly led her to schedule that first mammogram.

When the mammogram indicated a possible tumor, Angela next went to a surgeon for a needle biopsy. Angela recalls sitting in the waiting room at the oncologist's office with her husband awaiting the test results. She says it literally felt like a lifetime.

It was not good news. Angela was diagnosed with stage 2 breast cancer at just thirty-five. Her immediate reaction: *"This can't be happening to me!"*

Understandably she was in shock and shed tears at the news. That once nagging feeling that something wasn't quite right was now confirmed.

Angela's children were the driving force, the inspiration for her to get through and beyond this journey. *"I didn't have time to focus just on me"* she says. *"I had two children to be strong for. They needed me."*

Angela and her husband told their children the truth about what was going on, reassuring them that Mommy would get some medicine and would get better.

I believe we, as parents, need to instill confidence and reassurance in our children because they look to their parents for guidance and need that sense of security especially when dealing with difficult life circumstances. Angela laughs when recalling the response that let her know her son felt secure. He said, *"Can I still go to karate?"*

The next few weeks were a whirlwind of tests and scans to determine if the breast cancer had spread. Angela recalls feeling like she was in a fog and enduring several sleepless nights. She'd ask herself questions like *"What if it has spread?"* and *"Why did I wait to follow up?"*

Sadly the additional tests and scans confirmed that the breast cancer had spread to her lymph nodes. Angela was now in for a journey that would have her endure eight rounds of chemotherapy treatment, a double mastectomy, and reconstruction.

Even though the chemotherapy did cause Angela to lose her hair, she says, *"The fear of losing my hair was much worse than actually losing it."*

She tried to focus on being normal and didn't want people feeling sorry for her.

As Angela reflects on her journey, she recalls that her husband, Brian, was an absolute rock; and her neighbors and family were very supportive. Although she did not live locally, her mom visited often and was also a great support.

By the grace of God, Angela is here to share her story! *"God placed in my heart the desire to give back and help other women,"* she says.

Angela is such a brave young mom, who feels grateful to be here today. She encourages and helps other women through her business in her local community and elsewhere, by providing them with resources, tools, and information on breast awareness, self-exams, the importance of early detection, knowing the signs and symptoms of breast cancer, survivorship, and advocacy.

Today Angela is leading an active lifestyle, running her business, staying fit bike-riding several times a week, and making time to socialize with her friends. She is a breast cancer thriver and a proud mom to her now eleven- and fourteen-year-old children.

Now Angela's focus is on her overall wellbeing, taking care of her mind, body, and soul. She schedules timely follow-ups with her doctors and discusses any health concerns with them. Angela enjoys spending time with people who are uplifting. She has also learned to prioritize and say no to certain things. She chooses to be diligent when it comes to nutrition and fitness.

Angela believes that if we are granted more time, we should do all we can to use it wisely. She says, "*Giving and doing for others can be the best medicine for the soul when it's done from the heart.*"

To learn more about Angela you can visit her web site at:

www.breastinvestigators.com

Coaching Insights

1. What did you find most inspiring about Angela's story?

2. What was it about her attitude, faith, and mindset that stood out to you the most?

3. How is her story similar to yours?

4. How is it different?

5. What did you learn from reading her story?

6. What part of her story did you find uplifting and comforting?

7. What are the three biggest takeaways you got from her story?

Your Notes...

Do you not know that in a race all the runners run,
but only one gets the prize?
Run in such a way as to get the prize.
—1 Corinthians 9:24 (NIV)

SUZANNE

By stretching forth thine hand to heal;
and that signs and wonders may be done
by the name of thy holy child Jesus.
—Acts 4:30 (KJV)

CHAPTER 7

A WOMAN'S
CROWNING GLORY

SUZANNE'S STORY

S uzanne is a radiant, beautiful, and courageous woman of Catholic faith, who finds joy in classical music, gardening, and sewing. A lector for her church and former choir member, she is the go-to person to whom neighbors and friends turn whenever they have a problem.

She is a thirteen-year thriver of stage 2A breast cancer and was diagnosed at the age of fifty on October 19, 1998, a day she says she will never forget.

Originally from Pennsylvania, of Hungarian descent, Suzanne now lives in Florida with her husband, Jeff, and their ten-year-old rat terrier dog, Portia. Like many Europeans, she was raised on a hearty diet of meat and potatoes. She doesn't recall any family history of breast cancer.

Now sixty-four and the picture of health, Suzanne smiles at me across the table. I notice she's wearing a beautiful pink heart necklace and matching sweater that compliment her skin and hair tone beautifully.

Suzanne begins to share her journey through breast cancer, and her victory beyond as a 13-year thriver. She explains how she believes it was her upbeat attitude, faith, and positive visualization techniques that helped her kick breast cancer to the curb and thrive beyond it. I really love how she chose to see things in such a positive way, when she just as easily might not have given the circumstances. As we journey further back into Suzanne's story, she recalls learning that she had dense breasts in the early '70s when she was twenty-eight. At this time she discovered a lump in her left breast. She consulted a surgeon and underwent an excisional biopsy to remove the lump, which turned out to be benign. Suzanne then began having annual mammograms.

Suzanne's second experience with a lump in her breast - this time in the right breast - would prove much more serious. Discovering the lump while showering, she quickly visited her surgeon, who recommended that she eliminate caffeine from her diet and return after her next menstrual cycle. He explained that her breasts were lumpy and dense, which could be related to her cycle.

When she returned, the surgeon recommended an excisional biopsy; and she awoke from the surgery to learn she had stage 2A breast cancer. Her previous mammogram had shown no sign of the disease.

Suzanne recalls thinking, "*Why me? Why me?*" She felt alone, abandoned, and as though she was the only woman in the world with breast cancer.

Knowing her strength, Suzanne's husband told her, "*Why not you? You are strong; you can do this. We can tackle this together like any other problem.*"

With most of Suzanne's family living out of state, she knew she would have to pull herself up by the bootstraps and go to war against cancer.

Suzanne hardly remembers the first three days following her diagnosis. She went through the motions of daily life: cooking, cleaning, grocery shopping, and walking her dog. In fact caring for her thirteen-year-old chamois Beagle-Pomeranian mix was her salvation because the dog was also enduring a physical problem, a torn knee ligament. Suzanne chose not to focus all her attention on herself and her own set of circumstances. She had others dependent on her!

When Suzanne gave her sister-in-law, a clinical psychologist in Pittsburg, the news, her sister-in-law suggested reconstruction. She told Suzanne, "*You are too young to be without one of your breasts for the rest of your life.*"

Suzanne called her brother next, her only sibling. It was the hardest thing she had to do, she says, telling him his baby sister had breast cancer. She heard nothing and then a lengthy exhale on the other end, as if someone had punched her brother in the stomach.

Suzanne reminds us that cancer is something that affects the entire family, not only the patient. Everyone reacts differently to the situation.

Suzanne's surgery lasted five and a half hours, including a right-side mastectomy and reconstruction using tissue taken from her abdomen. In the days that followed, the nurses would get cross with her because she wouldn't stay in bed. She was eager to be up and around. Why doesn't this surprise me about Suzanne?

She excitedly remarks, "*A free tummy tuck!*"

Suzanne mentions a particular affirmation that helped her through her journey with breast cancer, one that she repeated over and over while walking two miles a day: "*Healthy am I, happy am I, holy am I.*"

She had chosen to speak positive words even though it was a challenging time, and she expected a great outcome.

Another positive and powerful visual Suzanne shares is that whilst she received chemotherapy treatments she would picture Pac-Man characters making their way one after another to eat the cells and destroy the disease. She would tell herself the red liquid injected into her body was like red Jell-O, in stark contrast to other patients referring to it as the red devil. Red Jell-O certainly sounds more appealing!

Suzanne shares a particular story from her journey that caused her to have a paradigm shift. She refers to it as, "*a woman's crowning glory.*"

Suzanne had been at the mall during her treatments and was not feeling or looking very well. She recalls frankly, "*I was having my own pity party. I felt piss-poor.*"

Then she saw a woman in a wheelchair who was using a blow tube to breathe. "*I felt like someone had just slapped me across the face,*" she says.

In that moment, Suzanne felt a complete shift in her perspective. She decided to take back control of her life. She went home feeling empowered and took action…shaving her head instead of waiting for her hair to fall out.

For Suzanne this was the right thing to do. You must do what feels right in your individual circumstances.

Suzanne says, "*It was a bold, brave, beautiful, and triumphant move!*"

She had taken a firm stand, a proactive approach that would help her deal with the disease her way.

Today, Suzanne shares with me the many blessings she has come to know as a result of going through and beyond her journey with breast cancer. She believes she is healthier today, having kicked cancer to the curb and is grateful for being given a second chance in life.

"I have a deeper appreciation for life," she says, *"and I am thankful for what I have."*

Suzanne mentions how very supportive her husband was throughout her journey, going with her to doctor visits and doing breast cancer research on the Internet. She also expresses gratitude to her friends and caregivers for their support.

Suzanne helps other women on their journey through breast cancer by volunteering with her local American Cancer Society Reach to Recovery program and the Look Good…Feel Better support program, which teaches women how to apply cosmetics and take care of their skin during their treatment.

In 2011 Suzanne received the State Sunrise Award for the Florida division of Look Good…Feel Better. An outstanding volunteer with the program for more than ten years, she was honored for her commitment, dedication, and encouragement to help women be the best they can be while living with cancer.

Suzanne advises, *"When you get up in the morning, even if you look in the mirror and feel or think you don't look good, say to yourself 'I feel good. I look good. I am good.'"*

Put on your moisturizer and lipstick, and pick out something vibrant to wear!

Suzanne's simple yet profound message to other women diagnosed with breast cancer is the title of a song she remembers hearing in the plastic surgeon's office: *"I will survive."*

Suzanne shares a visual healing exercise she learned at the local wellness support group, which she says helped her.

Lie quietly on the floor or on a recliner and close your eyes. Breathing in and out slowly, picture a walkway lined with flowers in every color of the rainbow. Each color represents a different affirmation. Red says to give and receive love. Orange is a reminder to eat healthy food. Yellow is a reminder to get plenty of sleep and relaxation. Green tells you to spend time outdoors. Blue says to engage in play and laughter. Purple tells you to nurture your spirit.

At the end of the pathway is a beach or another place that is special to you. You see a symphony orchestra and start conducting the classical music the orchestra is playing. After a while you slowly walk back up the path lined with flowers, feeling calm, refreshed, and serene.

Suzanne recalls coming back too quickly the first time and not wanting to leave her special and sacred place, but she knows it will always be there.

Suzanne's final message to you is, "*You must have hope! You can get back to normal, but it's a new normal. There is life after cancer. You are forever changed because of it, and in many ways you are better for it.*"

She says that this was her wake-up call to do and be more, to help and serve other women.

Coaching Insights

1. What did you find most inspiring about Suzanne's story?

2. What was it about her attitude, faith, and mindset that stood out to you the most?

3. How is her story similar to yours?

4. How is it different?

5. What did you learn from reading her story?

6. What part of her story did you find uplifting and comforting?

7. What are the three biggest takeaways you got from her story?

Your Notes...

So do not fear, for I am with you;
do not be dismayed, for I am your God.
I will strengthen you and help you;
I will uphold you with my righteous right hand.
—Isaiah 41:10 (NIV)

JAN

Then Jesus said to her,
"Woman, you have great faith!
Your request is granted."
And her daughter was healed at that moment.
—Matthew 15:28 (NIV)

CHAPTER 8

A TIME TO SERVE

JAN'S STORY

Jan is an attractive, athletic and upbeat blond haired lady of fifty-one, who earned her degree in education. She is a proud mother of two daughters Taylor and Megan. Jan is a woman of strength, who is thriving beyond her journey of stage 3 breast cancer. She was diagnosed at the age of forty-seven on Friday the 13th, just a few days following her grandmother's passing and the surgery of one of her daughters.

A woman of deep Catholic faith, Jan wears a beautiful graphite glass cross on a chain around her neck. It catches my attention as she smiles widely back at me across the table.

Our children are often our greatest inspiration in life, and that certainly is true for Jan. She says, "*My children were my biggest motivator. I had to be around for my two girls.*"

She herself grew up with six siblings in an athletic family that lived in rural Lake City in North Florida. To her knowledge there is no history of breast cancer in her family.

At the time of her diagnosis, Jan's immediate thought was of survival. All she wanted to know was, *"OK, so how do we fix it?"*

Jan continued to work throughout her journey with and beyond breast cancer. *"I did the best I could,"* she says. Her attitude and outlook in life has always been that the glass is half full, not half empty. She would do her best to stay positive.

Jan's breast cancer was located at the 9:00 o'clock position on her right side, and she learned that it was the size of a kiwi fruit.

Just a few hours before surgery, Jan recalls lying in the hospital bed and being told that she did not have medical insurance. She had recalled that an insurance agent had visited her at work one day and advised that she switch her current insurance. She hadn't realized at the time that the switch that had taken place was from a full-coverage policy to a supplemental one. Luckily her two sisters managed to gain coverage for Jan through Medicaid, so the surgery could go ahead as planned.

Following three hours in surgery and the removal of twenty-eight lymph nodes, Jan began her journey to recovery. She tells me how her faith, support network, and caregivers played such a huge and significant role towards her recovery. She also believes that her positive outlook in life truly helped.

While her surgery took place in Lakeland, Jan's medical records were originally in Sarasota. The MRI results hadn't moved from point a to point b until nine days following her surgery.

Once the records did arrive, she was now in for some additional news: there was another spot located at the 3:00 o'clock position, which had this been known prior to her surgery, would have dictated that a mastectomy be performed at that time.

At this unexpected news, Jan decided to attend a healing service in MacClenny, Florida. She tells me how she prayed and prayed and was blessed with holy water during this service.

The most wonderful news came next! Her new scan following the healing service showed the all clear. The spot that had been visible the first time around had now vanished. Jan feels incredibly blessed and grateful. *"My faith has helped me immensely, and it has been and still is my anchor,"* she says.

Next Jan would take on chemotherapy and recalls how she had prayed for nine days that she wouldn't lose her hair.

"The prayer helped me and armed me," she says of preparing for the journey that lay ahead.

At one of Jan's doctor visits, an oncology nurse showed her pictures of all the different kinds of wigs in a catalog. Jan recalls laughing and saying, *"Oh, I won't be needing one of those."* She later *realized there was a bigger plan at play, and there was absolutely no outsmarting it!*

Jan shares a funny memory with me about the day she and her new friend, Gina - also known as her new wig, were speeding down the street with Jan at the wheel and Gina sitting quietly in the passenger seat! Jan felt lucky to not get a speeding ticket and says *"There is compassion in the world, but it's not a freebie to speed."*

Jan's message to other women on their journey with breast cancer is *"You are going to be okay. It is a process, a journey."*

Today Jan is healthy and stays active playing tennis several times a week as the member of a tennis team. She presently works full-time in a barbershop and finds herself often giving others a word or two of encouragement about bad hair days.

Between work and tennis Jan also finds time to enjoy volunteering at the local Salvation Army. She says, *"It's a good way to give back, help, and serve others."*

Jan shares her love for making healing blankets as a way to provide comfort to other people who are also enduring medical challenges of their own, putting her entrepreneurial talents to great use whilst helping others. She finds this fulfilling and enjoyable. Jan is excited about this venture and looks forward to seeing her business grow while at the same time helping others.

Jan tells me, "*I am not a victim. This too shall pass.*"

I believe you should choose to see yourself as a victor not a victim. Often out of life's biggest challenges and difficulties, new blessings are born. Blessing that can help others in their hour of need!

Jan tells me that one of her blessings, as a result of her journey through breast cancer, is that she now sees things differently. "*It helps you put things into perspective,*" she says.

Jan shares a cute story about a gentleman who came into the barbershop and seemed overly concerned with his hair challenges. She smiled and reassured him, relating how she'd felt during the time she was a bald hairdresser. She definitely understood.

Another blessing Jan feels grateful for is the wonderful experience she had with her doctors, caregivers, and the rest of the medical team. She talks about how wonderful they were and how she really appreciated them.

She tells me another funny story about the time she was standing in line at the grocery store deli counter after having her chemotherapy and radiation treatment. This day she hadn't been wearing one of her colorful headscarves and was courageously sporting her cute new short hairdo. She was trying to reassure and convince herself that this new hairstyle was just the way she had chosen to wear her hair now. A gentleman approached her and said, "*Oh, I bet the hairdressers don't like you wearing your hair that short.*" Jan's reply came with a big, wide smile: "*Well, actually, I am a hairdresser; and this is a result of cancer and chemo.*" For obvious reasons she didn't go on a date with this gentleman. She laughs and reminds me that she used the term gentleman loosely!

Jan recalls how it would have been easy to let this man's negative remark get the better of her, but instead she felt that she should politely educate him. His remark had made him look like a fool.

Certainly Jan had to overcome the challenges she experienced along her journey with breast cancer, and I believe you can too. I love the fact that she chose to stay in faith, be positive, and keep her sense of humor throughout.

Jan has so much gratitude for the love and support she received from her children, her two sisters, and the rest of her family. It really helped her a lot on her journey.

Jan wins, game, set and match. So can you. Power up your attitude, stand in your greatness, and don't be afraid to show your moxie.

Coaching Insights

1. What did you find most inspiring about Jan's story?

2. What was it about her attitude, faith, and mindset that stood out to you the most?

3. How is her story similar to yours?

4. How is it different?

5. What did you learn from reading her story?

6. What part of her story did you find uplifting and comforting?

7. What are the three biggest takeaways you got from her story?

Your Notes...

LUANN

May the God of hope fill you with all joy and peace
as you trust in him,
so that you may overflow with hope
by the power of the Holy Spirit.
—Romans 15:13 (NIV)

CHAPTER 9

A HEART OF HOPE

LUANN'S STORY

Luann is a beautiful, blond, joyful, and positive woman. She served in the Army during Desert Storm, is a wife, and a mother to two girls and a boy. Now at the age of fifty-two, LuAnn, a woman of faith, a Christian Baptist, recalls how she was diagnosed with stage 3.5 triple-negative breast cancer in June 2009 at the age of just forty-nine.

LuAnn tells me how her Father was always such a positive man; she values this trait and takes after him. She had grown up in Illinois on 3.5 acres of land and was raised mostly on what she'd consider an organic diet. As we discuss family history, the only person she recalls having breast cancer was her maternal aunt.

LuAnn, an excited entrepreneur had no sooner opened the doors to her new business, a balloon decor store and would now be forced to close it down due to her unexpected diagnosis.

At the time she was diagnosed, she recalls wondering, "*Why me?*" followed by, "*It can't be real; it can't be happening.*" Then she'd felt a soft whisper, a voice inside her that said, "*Why not?*" Although LuAnn had managed to remain relatively calm upon receiving the news, her older daughter likely shed enough tears for both of them and understandably so.

LuAnn would later endure a lumpectomy. She says she was disappointed, then she chuckles. "*I was looking forward to a new set of boobs!*"

She explains that the chemotherapy would make her feel sleepy, so she would spend Saturdays in bed resting.

"*I don't know whether I forgot things because of the chemotherapy, a side effect often referred to as chemo brain,*" she says, "*or rather because I am blond.*"

It's interesting and uplifting how LuAnn chose to think of her circumstances, when she had every reason to view her situation in a less-than-positive way.

LuAnn recalls the sense of community she felt at her weekly visits for chemotherapy when she would see other women who were on similar journeys with breast cancer. She says, "*The coolest part is it's like you are in a club.*"

She would make it a point to stay positive, smiling, and being encouraging and having a good attitude toward those she met. LuAnn says she is grateful to the medical staff for doing such a wonderful job.

LuAnn shares a bold move she had taken during this time when she decided one day to take matters into her own hands. She shaved off her hair rather than wait for the possibility of it falling out by itself. She was blessed in time with thicker and curlier hair, something LuAnn was very happy about. She had taken a bold step and received a blessing in return.

She would delight in wearing hats and remarks, "*I actually think I looked good in a hat.*" She also had a scarf for every outfit in many different patterns and colors. LuAnn decided that she was going to wear her own style!

Her biggest support through her entire journey with breast cancer came from her church family, LuAnn recalls. She shares how extremely grateful she is to them for the support, outpouring of hugs, kind words, and love she received in her personal hour of need.

Today LuAnn stands tall as a beacon of hope for others. Members of her local church often point other women who have been diagnosed with breast cancer in LuAnn's direction, knowing she can give them hope and offer help on their journey.

LuAnn lives with her husband and their two dogs, Olive and Sport, in Sarasota. In her spare time, LuAnn loves kayaking, shopping, and reading. She works part-time in a local Christian bookstore.

She continues to bring joy to others through her talent and skill for clowning. She puts smiles on patients' faces in the local hospital with her creative balloon designs. In some cases these are the last colorful visuals a patient might see.

Another blessing LuAnn shares as a result of her journey through and beyond breast cancer is that she does more for herself now, whether it's treating herself to a manicure or catching a good movie.

"*Thank you God for not letting me die,*" LuAnn says.

She is grateful to her women-of-faith group for their support and comfort, which really helped her get through her journey with breast cancer. She didn't feel alone!

"You cannot quit; you have to persevere.

Have hope and try to have a positive attitude."

—LuAnn

Coaching Insights

1. What did you find most inspiring about LuAnn's story?

2. What was it about her attitude, faith, and mindset that stood out to you the most?

3. How is her story similar to yours?

4. How is it different?

5. What did you learn from reading her story?

6. What part of her story did you find uplifting and comforting?

7. What are the three biggest takeaways you got from her story?

Your Notes...

NORMA

I have fought the good fight,
I have finished the race,
I have kept the faith.
—2 Timothy 4:7 (NIV)

CHAPTER 10

A PILLAR OF STRENGTH

NORMA'S STORY

Norma is a beautiful and remarkable forty-six-years-young woman, a courageous mama bear with a love for photography and writing and a passion for travel. She is a two-year thriver of stage 4 breast cancer and a thriver beyond many other life circumstances as well.

A strong young woman of deep faith and Latin descent, Norma grew up in Miami and now lives in Sarasota. She was raised in the Catholic Church. Norma's inspiration and drive to thrive beyond her journey with breast cancer comes from her desire to see her boys grow up.

Norma shares how she had come away from the church earlier in her adult years and has since returned, this time on her terms and in a new environment. She says that her Christian faith, friends, and support groups have become her pillars of strength.

I notice her beautiful warm smile, and twinkly chocolate-brown eyes looking back at me across the table. Her periwinkle blue sweater is a perfect match for the bandana that allows only a glimpse of her brown hair.

The warm smile gradually reveals an enormous amount of endurance, persistence, faith, and hope as Norma shares with me her challenges over the past twelve months. This is a story that will inspire, provide hope, and encourage you on your journey.

It was January 2010 and Norma was newly married to Rick, the love of her life. Their journey as husband and wife had just begun, and the future looked bright. Now that she has endured the circumstances and chain of events that followed, Norma feels she is here today by the grace of God to tell her story.

Shortly after the wedding Norma's mother passed away, on January 20th. Just a two months later on March 26th, she was faced with her Father's passing. Certainly a difficult time in anyone's life to have two parents pass away in such a short amount of time of one another. As devastating as this was in some respects, Norma feels it was a blessing that her parents passed away when they did because seeing how much her cancer had affected her appearance would have been very difficult for them.

The news Norma received next, in May of the same year, revealed the cause of the twelve months of back pain she had already endured. Her husband and sister were with her when she received the news. Norma was diagnosed with stage 4 breast cancer, which had metastasized to her spine and ribs. She recalls hearing a quiet inner voice whispering, "*You will not die from this!*" The world as she knew it was now changed.

As a practical woman, Norma immediately wanted to know what the next steps were. The course of treatment prescribed for her was radiation followed by chemotherapy.

It was now September and Norma was glad to finally be home following a month in the hospital and two more months in rehab. The newlyweds had certainly endured a rollercoaster of events in their new journey together.

Norma had already endured much in such a short span of time, but she says, "*I do not bear a grudge. It was in God's hands.*"

On top of everything else, after five years of service to her employer, Norma lost her job. She was now faced with the challenge of fighting breast cancer with the expense of health insurance through her COBRA coverage. Norma says she was saddened when no one from the office had visited her since she left. Where were her former coworkers' compassion and caring during her time of need?

All of us hope that our partner and loved ones will be there for us in our time of need. Sadly this would not be the case for Norma. The love of her life, a strong man and former Marine, died of a heart attack in December that same year.

Here was Norma, barely able to take care of herself, and by the grace of God she got through this incredibly difficult time. She had become the rock when her family was no longer there to support her. She was now a sole survivor.

Today Norma delights in life and tells me of her dreams to write a book, to travel, and to help others. She has many beautiful destinations she wants to see and hopes one day to cycle again. This is an activity she loved, often cycling for 20 miles at time.

Norma's message to you is, "*Have the attitude to win, the faith and drive to move on.*"

"*Stay strong, be positive, and fight.*"
—Norma

Coaching Insights

1. What did you find most inspiring about Norma's story?

2. What was it about her attitude, faith, and mindset that stood out to you the most?

3. How is her story similar to yours?

4. How is it different?

5. What did you learn from reading her story?

6. What part of her story did you find uplifting and comforting?

7. What are the three biggest takeaways you got from her story?

Your Notes...

A cheerful heart is good medicine,
but a crushed spirit dries up the bones.
—Proverbs 17:22 (NIV)

CHAPTER 11

A CHAMPION'S
STUDY GUIDE

1. What did all seven women have in common besides breast cancer?
2. What did you find inspiring about their stories?
3. What were the positive daily affirmations Suzanne practiced on her daily walks?
4. Visually Suzanne chose to see her treatment in a positive way, how did she describe the chemo treatment?
5. What were the three important anchors Tammy shared in her story?
6. What was Norma's biggest pillar of strength?
7. In what ways is Jan helping, serving, and giving back as a result of coming through her journey?

8. What did LuAnn share as one of the blessings resulting from her journey?
9. What blessing did Martha receive as a result of her journey?
10. How is Angela helping other women on their journey through breast cancer?
11. What does God reward the crown of life for?
12. What tool did Tammy and her husband use that helped them share the news of her breast cancer with their child?
13. Whose story is similar to yours and why?
14. Whose story is least like yours and why?
15. Which story has inspired you the most and why?
16. What did Angela's son say after hearing that Mommy would be taking medicine to get better?
17. How did LuAnn and Suzanne take matters into their own hands?
18. Which woman's message resonates with you the most?
19. List five of your hearts desires, five things that you want to accomplish in life.
20. What metaphor does the book use to describe transition?
21. In what ways do you need to be the athlete in tackling your journey through breast cancer?
22. What kind of spirit does the book suggest you have?
23. What will you do to stay positive during a stormy season in your life?
24. Who in your life is uplifting, supportive, and caring?
25. Where can you search for more information about your circumstances?
26. Which woman in the book provides resources, information, and tools for other women with breast cancer?
27. Have you prayed boldly and asked Him for His favor today?

28. What was one of the blessings LuAnn mentions about her hair?

29. Does God have the power to heal? If you believe so, how do you know?

30. See yourself thriving beyond breast cancer and living your heart desires, accomplishing your goals in life. In five words describe how you will feel having achieved these things.

The Lord is my light and my salvation
whom shall I fear?
The Lord is the stronghold of my life
of whom shall I be afraid?
—Psalm 27:1 (NIV)

CHAPTER 12

❧

SEVEN "T'S TO THRIVING BEYOND
THE CROWN OF LIFE

1. Time For Healing
2. Thriving Beyond
3. Testing, Testing, 1-2-3...
4. Transformation and New Beginning
5. Treasuring and Cherishing
6. Trusting That It Will Be Done
7. Teaching, Leading, Serving

THE SEASONS OF LIFE
TIME FOR HEALING

a time to be born and a time to die
a time to plant and a time to uproot,
a time to kill and a time to heal,
a time to tear down and a time to build,
a time to weep and a time to laugh,
a time to mourn and a time to dance,
a time to scatter stones and a time to gather them,
a time to embrace and a time to refrain from embracing,
a time to search and a time to give up,
a time to keep and a time to throw away,
a time to tear and a time to mend,
a time to be silent and a time to speak,
a time to love and a time to hate,
a time for war and a time for peace.
—Ecclesiastes 3:2-8 (NIV)

THRIVING BEYOND

Therefore I tell you,
whatever you ask for in prayer,
believe that you have received it,
and it will be yours.
—Mark 12:24 (NIV)

Make the decision that you will thrive beyond your journey with breast cancer. Declare to Him that you are healed, you are whole, and you are living a blessed life and thriving beyond these circumstances.

Pray and see yourself already as you desire to be, leading a life accomplishing your heart's desires and thriving beyond breast cancer, as if it is already so.

See how the women in this book have been able to thrive on their individual journeys beyond breast cancer and have gone on to lead rich and fulfilling lives accomplishing their heart desires beyond breast cancer.

Their stories are here to inspire, give hope, belief, and encourage you on your journey and to show you that it is possible to live a blessed life and thrive beyond breast cancer. This is possible for you. Stay in faith.

You have learned how these everyday women have pressed forward through their individual journeys and how they have also moved beyond their circumstances. These women are servant leaders. They are helping, serving, and supporting other women along their journeys with breast cancer in their local communities and beyond.

Do your best to stay positive and expect the best outcome for yourself. Surround yourself with positive people, people who love and care for you, and who are supportive and uplifting.

Choose to see yourself thriving, living abundantly, healed, and beyond the breast cancer. Do not let your circumstances take away your hope, your heart's desires. Do not let it define you or defeat you.

There is life beyond breast cancer, stay in faith, pray and know that it is possible to thrive beyond it!

Be strong, courageous and determined to thrive beyond this stormy season. Stay in faith, believe that you will move forward beyond this and go on to achieve your heart desires and lifelong goals. Have faith that God will show His favor, bless you, and rain his blessings on you during this season. Be bold in your prayers to Him and ask Him for His favor.

Life is made up of different seasons. See yourself coming through and beyond this one, thriving and leading a blessed life.

When we watch the Olympic games on TV we mostly see the final performances, the moments when the athletes compete and the moments when they are awarded their medals. What we don't often see is the back story, the story showing the athletes' journeys, where they endure, sweat, shed tears, and persist through the pain and injury, pushing themselves farther ahead and enduring strict training to become champions.

You must become the athlete behind the scenes on your journey through breast cancer. Be determined to thrive, persevere, and cross that finish line without giving up. Focus on the finish line, accomplishing victory.

TESTING, TESTING 123...

Look up, not down. You are a Springboard Spirit. Realize you can bounce back from breast cancer and all of life's circumstances.

Just as a palm tree bends and withstands the storm without breaking, we all must bend to withstand and move beyond the stormy times.

Stay in faith, believe that He wants to turn your difficulties into gifts, and that what was meant to harm you He will use for your good. He wants to pay you back double.

Life is full of the different seasons. There comes a time for everything. You have thrived beyond your life's circumstances before. Even when you felt like the wind had been knocked out of your sails, you got back up, you got on course, you moved ahead in the right direction and reached the destination you desired.

Life is full of challenges, requiring us to take a seat, take stock, assess, and make necessary changes or adjustments to move on. Let God take the wheel. We don't always have to understand why things are the way they are; we must trust and have faith that He knows. He sees the complete masterpiece of our life. You and I only get a glimpse of the a partially complete masterpiece. It's only when we look back that we see all the dots connect.

Sometimes life throws us a curve ball when we least expect it. All of a sudden when things are going great, boom, we get knocked down. The great news is that we are like the palm tree. We bend and get back up. What is really important is that through the getting up we develop character. We spring forward and thrive. We become a Springboard Spirit, refusing to be defeated by the storms in life.

I understand that diagnosis, screenings, medical treatments, support, resources, care teams, and caregivers all play an important role toward your recovery. During this time of testing, I also believe you should get in agreement with God.

Expect the best outcomes and ask that He show you His favor. Declare to Him that you are healed, whole, and thriving beyond your journey with breast cancer.

It's through the difficult times and struggles we endure in life that we learn we must keep going, not letting our life's circumstances defeat us or define who we are. It's the character we develop through perseverance that produces hope. Yes, hope.

And hope does not disappoint us,
because God has poured out his love into our hearts by the Holy Spirit,
Whom he has given us.
—Romans 5:5 (NIV84)

TRANSFORMATION
AND
NEW BEGINNING

As the seasons change, from winter to spring, from spring to summer, summer to fall and fall to winter, we also find ourselves in constant change throughout our lives.

Our circumstances change, and we experience different seasons at different points in each of our lives. It is through these different seasons we find ourselves growing, changing, and evolving into the person we become, leaving behind our former selves and becoming a newer version, often an improved and even better version than before.

It is often after we endure the most difficult and challenging of times that we enjoy the beauty of new blessings, and new gifts.

Through these seasons we are tested, we persevere, we need patience, we learn, and we grow. There is a time for everything. You are in a season now during which you will need to be strong and courageous, to fight and not give up. In this season do your best to stay positive, expect the best, and have hope. Stay in faith.

You have learned through reading the seven women's stories in this book how their lives have been blessed beyond breast cancer. They share their gratitude for their newfound blessings and new perspectives on life, having come through the stormy season and victoriously crossed the finish line.

It's a time of rebirth, a time of renewal that's taking us from our old selves through a period of growth, change, and transition into our new selves. This is a time for shedding the layers of before and embracing new beautiful colors like that of a glorious butterfly.

The butterfly's spectacular colors are born from a process, a transition. She began as a small egg, became a caterpillar, then became a chrysalis, and finally became a bold and colorful butterfly, releasing her beauty, radiance, and renewed spirit as she flies and soars to new heights.

TREASURING
AND
CHERISHING

The Crown of Life is one of the crowns God rewards. He shows His favor upon those persevering under trial, patiently enduring, testing, and achieving victory. He delights in placing the crown on His daughter's head to reward her. The crown is worn to symbolize honor, victory, and glory.

I believe He is holding your crown in His hands, waiting to place it upon your head to honor you as you persevere through and endure patiently your journey beyond breast cancer.

In the ancient Olympic games, held in Olympia, Greece, the athletes were honored, praised, and celebrated for their victories and accomplishments and were rewarded with an olive branch crown. Interestingly one of the first games to take place was a foot race where young women competed for a position of high importance and honor. They competed not just for the sake of competing but to win.

In life, you must also be in it to win, to accomplish victory. Become a victor not a victim. Do not give up, but press on despite the challenges you are facing, and give it your best shot.

In a race all runners must run purposefully in a predetermined direction and with a heart of desire to win. Each year we see thousands of women walk around the country to raise funds that help fight against breast cancer. They walk to win, to cross the finish line. That is what you must do. Walk to win and set your sights on crossing the finish line. See yourself beyond the finish line, thriving and living your life's desires beyond breast cancer.

Certainly there are times in all our lives when we feel we are being tested, challenged, and pushed farther than we think we can go. These are the times that really call forth our patience, perseverance, and endurance to stay in hope and faith.

This is also a time to remain in agreement with God, a time to trust Him because He has a purpose and a plan for your life.

Be like the athlete. Run with purpose to win. Focus your sights on becoming a victor, crossing that finish line and seeing yourself crowned for all that you have endured, for the patience and persistence you have shown, and for your accomplishment, your victory, your win.

The Greeks believed that the ancient Olympic games would bring peace and harmony and that there is a relationship between worship and athletics. Be the athlete, have faith, and ask God for His favor. Be bold and ask Him to rain on you during this season and declare to Him your heart's desire to thrive beyond your journey.

I believe He wants to favor you with a crown, the crown of life, as one of his daughters who has persevered beyond the challenges and one who has endured pain and suffering along the way. Be bold, be brave, be beautiful because you are!

TRUSTING
THAT
IT WILL BE DONE

She is clothed with strength and dignity;
she can laugh at the days to come.
—Proverbs 31:25 (NIV)

Trust and believe you can go higher, you can rise taller and live a life thriving beyond breast cancer. Be in faith. Trust that God wants you to thrive.

Believe you are healthy, whole, and living well beyond this disease. Believe that He will show up in your life in extraordinary ways because He wants to make you an example of His goodness. When he does this, it honors Him.

Be still because there is no fear in faith.

Trust that He has you in the palm of his hand and that He wants you to thrive and not simply survive. Stay in faith, in peace and think positively. Have a Springboard Spirit, and believe you will flourish. Trust in Him.

He said to her,
"Daughter your faith has healed you.
Go in peace and be freed from your suffering."
—Mark 5:34 (NIV)

TEACHING, LEADING, SERVING

When he had finished washing their feet,
he put on his clothes and returned to his place.
"Do you understand what I have done for you?" he asked them.
"You call me 'Teacher' and 'Lord,' and rightly so, for that is what I am.
Now that I, your Lord and Teacher, have washed your feet,
you also should wash one another's feet.
I have set you an example that you should do as I have done for you."
—John 13:12-15 (NIV)

We are sisters, you and I. We are the same. You are not better or less than I. I am not better or less than you. We are in this boat together and not on individual islands by ourselves; we are all connected. All of our positive and negative life experiences become part of our whole being and the person we become after we go through and beyond them. We are here to serve and help each other.

It is my belief we are all here for a purpose, a purpose far greater than ourselves. We are here to serve and help one another. I do not believe in coincidences. I think people come in and go out of our lives for a specific reason. We are like an incomplete jigsaw puzzle with the Master holding the missing piece that He will later reveal.

Serving others first requires putting the needs of others ahead of our own and staying in obedience to His will so that we can help and make a difference in their lives. With our love for humanity we are able to show our compassion, love, and empathy for others. We must listen and keep our hearts open, not casting judgment upon others and their ways. We do not know of their life experiences or what trials they may have endured along their journeys. After all, who are we to judge when we are all guilty of sin?

Since we are all in this boat together, I believe we should help and serve one another; and together we can help masses of people all around the world by sharing our love, compassion, and wisdom in obedience to His will.

We are all thriving in some way beyond our life experiences. God wants to turn around the hurts and disappointments we have endured and use them for good in our favor. The women whose stories are in this book and I are here to help and serve you on your journey. It is our hope that you will find these stories inspiring, and a source of hope and encouragement..

What greater way is there to glorify God than to do pleasing work, serving others and doing what's right? We show him our eternal gratitude for the favor He showed us by giving us more time, more time to serve and help one another in this world.

His calling to me was to go out and help millions of women and girls all around the world. I did not know how or what that would look like, yet I believed and trusted Him. I stay in faith with an open heart and await His call.

"This is your time.
This is your time to thrive.
This is your time to thrive beyond breast cancer..."
—Janet I. Mueller

CHAPTER 13

A CHAMPION'S GUIDE TO THRIVING BEYOND

I can do all this through him who gives me strength.
—Philippians 4:13 (NIV)

1. Stay in faith.
2. Pray daily.
3. Read your Bible daily.
4. Focus on reading healing scriptures.
5. Look ahead and see yourself thriving beyond breast cancer.
6. Do your best to focus on the joys in life and your most joyful memories.
7. Do not let this season steal your joy.

8. Keep your big vision and long-term goals in clear sight.

9. Choose to see this season as a speed bump and believe you will thrive beyond it.

10. Surround yourself with those who are kind, loving, supportive, and uplifting.

11. Do not let this season defeat you or define you.

12. Do not let this season defeat you.

13. Believe this too shall pass and focus on thriving.

14. Look at photographs of you. at your most radiant and healthy; place them somewhere you can see them daily.

15. See these pictures and believe you will be restored.

16. Keep a daily journal and include three things you are grateful for each day.

17. Journal at least one positive word, action, or conversation daily.

18. Journal your three most important long-term goals.

19. Think about how your journey beyond breast cancer can help someone else.

20. Think about how your experience could help others in their time of need.

21. Choose to see your treatments as a positive step toward healing.

22. Find one encouraging or inspiring piece of information from each story in this book.

23. Think about what blessings have been noted in the stories these women have shared as a result of their journey beyond breast cancer.

24. Be hopeful and believe that you will be healed and thrive beyond breast cancer.

25. Embrace all the care and medical help you can and partner with your care teams; expect a great outcome for yourself.

26. Look forward to a new you, a new season, and a new beginning.

27. Know that God wants to show His favor, that He is merciful and compassionate, and that He heals. He is supernatural.

CONCLUSION

In closing, my hope and prayers are that you are healed. That you find peace, comfort and hold onto your joys in life through this stormy season. Have a Springboard Spirit and let His love pour into you. Lean into Him and let Him show His favor, you are a child of God, you are His daughter and He loves you.

With Love and Healing

In prayer,

Dear Heavenly Father, You have the power to heal and restore. We pray that you will do now that which you have done before. We ask you dear Father to provide comfort and peace to all your daughters and in Jesus' name we pray that you provide healing to this woman and to all women around the world. Let them feel your love and arms around them, carrying them through and beyond this stormy season. Let them receive your healing in all ways spiritually, emotionally, physically, and mentally. You are a never changing God. I know that through you Lord Almighty all things are possible. AMEN

FOR HIS GLORY

ACKNOWLEDGEMENTS

I am deeply blessed and eternally grateful to God for His favor. I feel blessed that He gave me a passport to live beyond my near-death-experience. I am grateful to Him for giving me more time on this earth to help and serve others. I am deeply blessed for His guidance in writing this book and for the doors He opened. I am most grateful that he blessed my life with a beautiful friend whose life inspired this book.

Mom, Dad, and Darren, I am grateful for our family. I've witnessed and learned compassion, empathy, and caring for others. I'm grateful to you for teaching me values that have gone on to serve me in life. To my husband, Eric, thank you for your help and support. I cherish our life together. To Gennie, my mother-in-law, thank you for the hours you were available to spend with your granddaughter so I could complete this book.

I am blessed and grateful to the seven courageous champions, the women who have shared their stories in this book: Tammy, Martha, Angela, Suzanne, Jan, LuAnn, and Norma. It is my belief their stories will inspire, give hope, and encourage women around the world through and beyond their journey with breast cancer.

I am grateful to my friends for your love and friendship and to all who have been encouraging throughout writing this book.

To my dear friends back in the United Kingdom, Debbie Cook, Claire Kelley, Michaela Ransley-Simpson, Stuart Wheeldon, Colin Ludden, and Dominic Robinson thank you for your continued friendship and love over the years and across the miles.

My deepest gratitude to Terry Whalin for championing my message and to David Hancock, Rick Frishman, Margo Toulouse, Bethany Marshall and the entire family at Morgan James Publishing.

I am blessed and grateful for the many teachers and mentors who have influenced and touched my life: Del Gilfillan, Pat Lutz, Steve Mitten, Chris Barrow, Dr. John C. Maxwell, Tony Robbins, Darren Hardy, Brendon Burchard, Debbie Ford, Deepak Chopra, Marcia Wieder, Thomas Bähler, Barbara De Angelis, Marci Schimoff, Randy Gage, Jack Canfield, and Brian Tracy.

Brendon Burchard, deserves special credit here for inspiring excellence and encouraging me to share my voice, gifts, and message with the world to help improve the lives of many. I am most grateful. I have a deep burning desire and passion to pay this forward and help other people share their voices, gifts, and messages with the world too.

Tony Robbins, your heart to help and heal is beautiful. I'm so grateful to you for your mentoring in my life. I believe we are all here to serve a higher purpose, to turn our challenges into gifts so we can serve more fully, helping to heal the hearts of many around the world.

Dr. John C. Maxwell, my deepest gratitude to you for your leadership lessons and for inspiring me to always strive to be an excellent leader so I can continue helping others develop and rise up and be excellent leaders. Thank you for your ongoing inspiration and teachings that have impacted my life and leadership journey for more than fifteen years and will continue to do so.

Darren Hardy, I am most grateful to you for your encouragement, your high performance mentoring, and for inspiring and demanding the best in me and all those you serve. Thank you for the valuable lessons you share from those who are helping to improve the lives of many in the world.

I am grateful to Dr. Maria Mallarino for taking the time to meet with me and for sharing your vision, the needs and insights on a global perspective. With gratitude to the Living Word bookstore in Sarasota, FL for sharing a space for some of our interviews and to your amazing staff who provided such excellent customer service to me on my frequent and lengthy visits.

Thank you to Andrea Feldmar at the Center for Building Hope for allowing us to conduct our group interviews in your location.

To Rhonda and Shanan, I acknowledge you and thank you for your willingness to share your stories. God bless you.

ABOUT THE AUTHOR

 **Janet I Mueller** is the Founder of Leadership In Excellence Academy. She is a life and business development coach, speaker, and author. Janet is hired for her expertise to speak around the world on personal transformation and leadership development. She is also an advocate and speaks out on issues affecting women and girls including breast cancer, bullying and overcoming adversity.

Janet has appeared on both local and national TV including, SNN 6, ABC 7 MySuncoast, and Daytime NBC.

For more than twenty years Janet's leadership expertise, study of human psychology, and her gift for coaching has helped her to inspire, teach, and transform the lives of her clients and entrepreneurs worldwide. She has successfully led, coached and trained executive sales teams in the healthcare industry, and spent almost a decade leading teams with fortune 500 and 100 companies in the direct sales industry. Janet partners with organizations, teams and individuals inspiring and teaching them how to achieve higher levels of business growth, leadership development and personal performance.

Janet is grateful to God for giving her a passport to more time so she can continue to help and make a difference touching and transforming lives all around the world through her speaking, teaching, coaching, seminars and books.

A MESSAGE FROM THE AUTHOR
YOUR CHALLENGES
CAN BECOME
YOUR GREATEST GIFTS

Certainly there is hope today. There is light, kindness, and compassion available to all of us. There is healing, renewing, softening, and transformation. I believe we are all here to make a difference by sharing our unique gifts and purpose with the world. That each of us has a unique calling, a message, a purpose to fulfill. A seed planted in each of our hearts being nurtured, equipped, and ready to blossom. A seed positioned intentionally by our creator, for me, I believe God.

Now is the time we will see a rising of leaders who demonstrate and feel compassion and empathy. Leaders who have the courage to stand. Let us also be reminded of the courage, strength, resilience and endurance of the human spirit present in each and every one of us, in our communities, and in everyday messengers. How beyond difficulty and challenge we see a rising up and overcoming of adversity. We see gifts born out of struggle being used for good, for the greater and higher purpose to serve all. This book is an example of this and it shows us how these 7 courageous women through the healing of the mind, body and soul are now thriving beyond breast cancer. Be encouraged that you too can rise up and beyond adversity just as these 7 women and I have done.

I felt called to write this book, inspired by the loss of my best friend to breast cancer and having personally survived a near death experience. I believe I was given a passport to more time.

During the creation of this book I experienced a transcendence, a spiritual enlightenment. I feel called to serve, help, heal, inspire, teach and transform millions of lives all around the world. I came to understand in the most spiritual and profound way that it is possible for each of us to rise up and thrive beyond the adversities in each of our lives and to use these experiences for good. My challenge to you is this... To choose to see your adversity as a gift and to use this gift to serve and help others. I believe I live my message or as Mahatma Gandhi said *"My life is my message"* and certainly for each of us our life experiences could be our message, our purpose to fulfill, our gifts to share with the world; to use them for the greater good of all, and to heal the hearts of many.

My call to you is this...
LOVE · SERVE · LEAD
MAKE A DIFFERENCE, LEAVE A LEGACY™

Meet Janet and learn more about her seminars, and programs at
www.JanetIMueller.com

RESOURCES

American Cancer Society
250 Williams Street NW
Atlanta, Georgia, 30303
Toll-Free: 800-227-2345
www.cancer.org

Balloons That Bloom
Sarasota, FL
Phone: (941) 928-7638
balloonsthatbloom@yahoo.com
www.balloonsthatblom.com

Breastcancer.org
7 East Lancaster Avenue
3rd Floor
Ardmore, PA 19003
www.breastcancer.org

Breast Cancer Partner
info@breastcancerpartner.com
www.breastcancerpartner.com

Breast Investigators
www.breastinvestigators.com

Cancer Support Community
1050 17th Street, NW
Suite 500
Washington, DC 20036
Phone: (202) 659-9709
Toll-free: (888) 793-9355
www.cancersupportcommunity.org

Center for Building Hope
5481 Communications Parkway
Sarasota, FL 34240
Phone: (941) 921-5539
www.centerforbuildinghope.com

Center for Disease Control and Prevention
1600 Clifton Rd. Atlanta, GA 30333
Toll-free: (800) CDC-INFO (800-232-4636)
www.cdc.gov/cancer/breast/

Florida Cancer Specialists
600 N Cattlemen Rd, #200
Sarasota, FL 34232
Phone: (941) 377-9993
www.flcancer.com

Emerging Med
247 W. 30th Street
4th Floor
New York, NY, 10001
Toll-free: (877) 601-8601
www.emergingmed.com

Gerson Institute
3844 Adams Avenue
San Diego, CA 92116
Toll-free: (800) 838-2256
Phone: (619) 685-5353
www.gerson.org

Imerman Angels
400 W. Erie Street, Suite #405
Chicago, IL 60654
Phone: (312) 274-5529
www.imermanangels.org

KidsHealth – from Nemours
www.kidshealth.org/kid/grownup/conditions/breast_cancer.html

LiveStrong
2201 E. Sixth Street
Austin, TX 78702
Toll-free: (877) 236-8820
www.livestrong.org

Living Beyond Breast Cancer
354 West Lancaster Ave., Suite 224
Haverford, PA 19041
Phone: (610) 645-4567
www.lbbc.org

Look Good...Feel Better
c/o Personal Care Products
Council Foundation
1101 17th Street NW Suite 300
Washington, DC 20036
Tel: 202-331-1770
www.lookgoodfeelbetter.org

H. Lee Moffitt Cancer Center & Research Institute
12902 Magnolia Drive
Tampa, FL 33612
Toll Free: (888) MOFFITT (888-663-3488)
www.moffitt.org

National Breast Cancer Coalition
1101 17th Street, NW, Suite 1300
Washington, DC 20036
Phone: (202) 296-7477
Toll-free: (800) 622-2838
www.breastcancerdeadline2020.org

The Breast Cancer Research Foundation
60 East 56th Street
8th floor
New York, NY 10022
Toll-free: (866) FIND-A-CURE (866-346-3228)
www.bcrfcure.org

Susan G. Komen for the Cure
5005 LBJ Freeway, Suite 250
Dallas, TX 75244
Toll-free: (877) GO-KOMEN (877-465-6636)
www.komen.org

WebMD
www.webmd.com/breast-cancer

CPSIA information can be obtained at www.ICGtesting.com
Printed in the USA
BVOW07s1516190913

331630BV00004B/110/P